HEART,
HOME &
HARD HATS

To Georgiana
from Sur Cara
6-8-95

Also by Sue Doro

OF BIRDS AND FACTORIES

HEART, HOME & HARD HATS

The non-traditional work and words of a woman machinist and mother

by Sue Doro

MIDWEST VILLAGES & VOICES
3220 10th Avenue South
Minneapolis, MN 55407

Some of these poems have appeared in the
following publications:

AMMO, UNION WAGE, QUINDARO,
M. MAGAZINE FOR GENTLE MEN,
MAIN TREND, PRIMIPARA, BREAK
TIME, SACKBUT REVIEW, WOMEN:
A JOURNAL OF LIBERATION,
THE FIVE PETALED BLOSSOM,
THE MACHINIST, THE MILL HUNK
HERALD, TALKIN' UNION,
WORKING CLASSICS, FORWARD
MOTION, BROOMSTICK, VILLAGE
VOICE, TRADESWOMAN

(See last page for publication addresses.)

Sue Doro's poems were also included in
WOMEN BRAVE IN THE FACE OF
DANGER: PHOTOGRAPHS AND WRITINGS
BY LATIN AND NORTH AMERICAN WOMEN,
ed. Margaret Randall, 1985, The Crossing
Press, Trumansburg, NY 14886.

Printed by Thomas Printing, Minneapolis, MN
Titles typeset by Duck Type, Minneapolis, MN
Layout by Pat Kaluza
Cover by Marilyn Lindstrom

ISBN: 0-935697-01-2

Library of Congress Catalog Number:
86-162211

Printed in the United States of America

Preface

Carry this book around with you. Take it to union meetings, to your place of worship, give it to your neighbor or co-worker, read it aloud to the children. Go from door to door.

For here is a woman, a worker and a writer, who, out of the silencing, is speaking of what is really happening to us all--at home, at work, in the struggle. And you will find out how much of human experience has been silenced.

You will realize that there is no history of women told by themselves, that we have been portrayed in reduced images of our beauty and our strength, that we have even been made invisible.

That is why Sue Doro is to me a woman, a poet and a wonder. I know how it is to try and be a human being, blooming richly with a relationship, children, work and, after everyone is asleep, to make some marks on the cave walls, write something down, a message, a communication, an act of solidarity.

And Sue Doro has been to me a source of power and love. She uses the experiences of the working class as the root and flower of her perception. She is without hesitancy, inferiority or timidity, rising clear, serene in the criminal world of power and destruction, asserting among the ruins the clear, human solidarity with others, in a world that must not be destroyed.

Much of our culture is of death, alienation, inevitability of destruction, entire global ruin. For a number of years she has given to me courage and belief again in bread and roses, work and peace, the common experience and the common humanity coming into our common fate.

So that's why I say: give this book like bread and roses. It will be an anathema to those who plan our ruin and destruction. This is the best weapon against the destroyers, an image of relationship again, perpetual and excessive and generous in the people.

For it is only in those who make life and work that life's value is held, defended, protected and made visible.

Let this song go from hand to hand, heart to heart.

Meridel Le Sueur

From
Midwest Villages & Voices

This is Midwest Villages & Voices' second publishing venture, the second time we as a group have said we are responsible for our culture, for our community, and this is how in part we will fulfill that responsibility.

We believe that everything we do and experience is an expression of our culture and that we are all artists capable of sharing beautifully, uniquely that culture. That which recognizes us, inspires us, strengthens us is community. It is within our culture and our community that we find the meaningfulness of our lives.

Culture is not distant from us, too grand and sophisticated for us. Our culture is one patch of an infinitely varied patchwork quilt. Let us claim our share of that quilt--let us celebrate it, share it, grow from it. Let us be responsible for it.

This book of poems by Sue Doro is an expression of our culture and springs from our community--she speaks for us and to us, bringing us the world anew yet again. We are both proud to be the publisher and facilitator of HEART, HOME & HARD HATS and humble enough to know that if we can do it so can others.

Let the voice of the people be heard!

Meridel Le Sueur
Rachel Tilsen
Pat Kaluza
Gayla W. Ellis
David Tilsen

Contents

This book is dedicated to my family
at home and at work
especially Larry, my partner
these last fourteen years
for his beautiful constant support
in child-raising and writing.

With special thanks to Meridel Le Sueur,
friend and sister,
without whose help and encouragement
this book would not have been published.

1

Poet at Work
Milwaukee Road Railroad

the factory window
the factory
the window
the wind
trying to blow in

a poet tries to blow into your window
the poem is wind
tickling hair on the back of your neck

it cools
it freshens
it tries to dry the sweat
that's dripping down your face
before you blink
before the salt sweat
stings your eyes

you stop the machine you're running
turn and walk to the open window
you take your safety glasses off
and wipe your eyes and forehead
on your shirt sleeve

this moment is yours
to keep
to share
to smell
to see the daisies blowing
in the summer wind
by the edge of the railroad track

the factory's at your back
the poet in you helps this moment
live a little longer

she laughs
holding wind in her hands

Where's My Hammer?

number 13's still screwed up
have to whap it with a hammer
every time I want the tool bar up or down
and my arm is killing me
hammering at a funny sideways angle
all the time
told the foreman the machine was broke
he says it'll get fixed
it's on the "list"
felt like tellin' him
I got a list too...
and HE'S on it
WHERE'S MY HAMMER!?!

The Father Poem

my father,
dark gray,
dusty factory father,
left with only one lung
from filthy air,
aching with rheumatism,
from winter cold air
blowing on a sweaty body,
and sweltering and gasping
for breath in the summer months.

my father, cursing your job,
through us,
your family,
being mean to my mother,
to my brother, my sister,
to me.
yelling, coughing.
spitting yellow, green and red.

my father swallowing pills
to keep on your feet.
swallowing pills
to get to sleep.
my father,
two months into retirement,
the uncashed check
on the kitchen table,
found dead,
by the lady who ran
the downstairs tavern.

my father, dead,
your body melting
into the floor boards
near a shoe box
of assorted pills,
an empty brandy bottle,
and a bucket of spit
lined with newspaper.
your pain is finished now.

my father, dead but not gone,
alive but not living,
I remember you,
coming home
from a ten-hour work day,
taking off your glasses
to show white circles
of sunken eyes
surrounded by soot,
because sometimes
you were too tired
to clean up at work,
in the washroom
that your union fought for.

on those nights,
I remember
when the white circles
were around your eyes,
and your clothes
smelled like johnnie's bar,
you'd spit on the floor
and at momma,
and throw money at her,
and she would pick it up,
and put it in her apron pocket,
and you would swear
and yell at her
for being there,
and I would stand
around the doorway,
not wanting to leave her
alone with you,
but too afraid
to stand next to her
and fight.

my father,
dead but not gone,
alive but not living,

who were you?
some lost year on the farm,
when you were a little boy,
some summer gone loving
in the sun with my mother.
then in harder times,
driving your father's poultry truck
to milwaukee, loaded with
sand-stuffed chicken bodies,
to make them weigh more when you
        got there.

were you always mean?
or were there days
that I never knew?
old days, when you were the man
my mother loved,
before you worked
in a rich man's factory,
when both of you were young and new
and lived in berlin, wisconsin,
and went to band concerts in the park,
and gathered hickory nuts,
and knew everyone,
and always had enough to eat,
because "at least there was the garden,
and grandpa's farm, and potatoes in
        the cellar"
and the neighbors who shared what
        they had.

what did you feel
when the depression
stole your little business?
how scared were you
to come to a big city
with a wife and three babies?
how crazy did it make you
to be a family provider
who could not provide
in a system that demands it
as part of manhood?

my father,
a good welder,
proud to be
one of the best
in your department,
welding the seams
of giant blue corn silos
for farms you would only dream of,
and frames for trucks
you could never afford.
how did it feel
when a time came,
and your shaky hands
couldn't keep the torch steady,
and your watering eyes
wouldn't let you weld a straight line.

on the day you collapsed at work,
the shop doctor okayed
a week of sick leave,
and when you returned,
you found you'd been transferred
to the tool crib.
you were finished as a welder,
and now your job was
to hand others their tools.

you were old at fifty-five,
and I feared and hated
and did not understand you.
did you feel bad
when you cursed me
for not emptying your bucket
fast enough?
did you feel bad
when you cursed and blamed me
for momma's dying,
and for your son's death?
and for not being able
to breathe or hear or see
or walk without a cane?

you'd come home
to sit in your red rocker
by the window,
looking out on lisbon avenue,
and you'd rock and talk
to yourself
about corn silos,
soft winds,
and dead relatives.
what did you see
out the window?
how did you feel?
who were you?
questions you'll never
answer for me.
I'll never know.

the person my mother loved
in that little wisconsin town,
I'll never know,
because you were stolen
from my time of living
by profit-hungry factory owners,
who must be dealt with,
bosses who will be dealt with,
so people like you
won't have to die
in little dusty rooms,
alone, and never known
by people like me
who should rightly love
and just as rightly
fight side by side,
not against,
people like you.

my father,
dark gray,
dusty factory father,
dead but not gone,
alive but not living,
for thirty years
you had a clock number,
a.o. smith company
knew you by it.

I knew you
by the meanness
that the rich man drove you to.

you taught me that.
and now,
my dusty factory friend,
I'm learning
how to use that anger well
against the ones
that taught it best
to you.

Ours

they can't take the sky away
we know it's outside
though eyes see only
metal work pieces
going round and round
in the machines we run
and daylight filters in
through dark blue slits
of wired windows

they can't take the wind away
we know it's still there
flying across the parking lot
though the only breeze we feel
is our own air blowing
from lower lips
onto sweaty faces
as we work the line

they can't take the land away
it waits for us here under the bricks
of this factory building
owned by sick old dinosaurs
heaving their last stinking breaths

we are like the sky and the wind
watching over our land
making plans to bury the dinosaurs

we are this poem
that cannot be taken away
that cannot
be taken
away

2

Paper Napkin Poem for Larry

i am writing on a paper napkin
missing you   it is after lunch
and i am waiting for a 1:30 class

i am a 37 year old school "girl"
waiting for a 1:30 afternoon
industrial math class
and missing you

for five hours this morning
i faced and turned a steel bar
to specified length
on an engine lathe
and only thought about you
in between cuts
which is right and proper
and especially safe
considering the machine parts
were spinning
at 620 revolutions per minute

so you can see
now that i'm waiting
for my 1:30 math class to start
i can spend time safely
thinking about you
loving you
and feeling good
about my life and ours
while writing
this paper napkin love poem

The Little Engine Lathe Blues

one thousand
and five hundred times
today
i picked
put
sawapped
caranked
swatched
switched
turned
tossed
cranked
and stopped
to measure
every fifteenth
piece
to ninety-three
thousandths
of an inch
averaging out
to about
four a minute
or the reading
of this poem
constantly
for nine hours
averaging out
to fifteen
hundred
identical ways
to drive a person
crazy
just what it seems
capitalism
is trying
to do
to us

The Coil Winder

Beatrice the coil winder
brushes her teeth ten times a day

management does not care
because Beatrice winds coils
faster than anyone ever hired
for the job

Beatrice swallows pills
almost as often as she brushes her teeth

she's grateful for the job
management has given her

she winds coils faster and faster

brushes her teeth more and more

swallows her valiums and methedrines
with tranquil speed

and talks to no one

Beatrice the coil winder
doesn't remember how

Assembly Room Women

blue net caps on heads
bent over tables
covered with trays
of wire springs
thousands
of tiny copper coils
curling in piles
near hundreds of
boxes of metal brushes
endless numbers
of little two inch
squares
each needing
a wire spring
attached
each needing soldering
needing counting
needing boxing
needing the
assembly room women
to complete
their
creation

Cutting Room Men

gray dust spinning 'round their heads
whine of band saws penetrating bodies

Black and Chicano workers
cut chunks of carbon steel
into smaller and smaller hunks

no one even hears the scream
when Big Bird's finger is slashed
trying to push the last little piece
through the revolving blade

and dark-skinned fingers
bleed red blood
brown hands wipe the table
and the machines keep running

Carlos's ordered in from the warehouse
and Big Bird stops his own bleeding
with a shop rag

while Sam the foreman
watches with a white-faced frown
thinking of the trouble
of writing his report

"just another case of worker negligence,
of course"

Billy

hired yesterday
in this non-union shop
he was here

today he's gone
fired on the spot
by his foreman
ten minutes into
the first shift

for making a soundless
but articulate gesture
at the factory owner's
back

and for being
Black

Poem Too Tired for a Title

for Sue Silvermarie, poet and mail carrier

tired
as a
crumpled
lunch bag
home
after work
the factory's
sting
in my ears
i try
to smooth
myself
out
flatten
my wrinkles
and snap
myself
back into
life

The Judge

the day i went to court
to see real amerikan justice
working for me

judge seraphim wore a
yellow and green seersucker
striped sports coat
and a green tie

and he sentenced
an unemployed man
to 90 days
in the house of correction

to correct himself
for having stolen
a pair of shoes

then
he sent a young woman
to tacheta for 90 days
for shoplifting food
from the a&p
for her baby
because she had no money
to feed him and
she wasn't getting welfare and
her husband was in the brig
at great lakes and
the judge gave the courts custody
of the baby

all this and more
in a ten minute time span
from a yellow and green
seersucker
whose turn will come

whose turn will come

his turn will come

Muscle

Listen!
This is a muscle poem.
Its sounds are loud
and can be frightening
to untrained ears.

It smells of oil
and sweaty T-shirts,
and steel shavings,
and cleaning compound
on concrete floors.

But for those
who understand,
this poem wears
safety glasses
and steel-toed boots
filled with pride and love.

As to those people
who are only moved
by greed and profits,
I want these words
to drop on them
like a load of steel bars
from a hundred feet
in the air!

3

Ruthie

whenever i travel through
my old neighborhood on the northside,
i think of eyedie,
and when i think of ruthie,
i hear her LAUGH!

ruthie! she sure could laugh!

one time we were practicing basketball
after school
in the old saint thomas aquinas gym,
her and mary ellen and i,
when ruthie slipped and
tripped on her own foot.
she started to laugh,
sitting on the floor where she fell,
laughing and holding the basketball
against her belly.
laughing so hard,
tears were dripping from her eyes.
mary ellen and i were laughing too,
just watching ruthie laugh,
when a little river of something wet
began to grow under ruthie,
it trickled and weaved its way
across the old wooden floor
like a grass snake,
and three crazy twelve year old girls
        eyed it,
giggling and gasping for air
on the basketball court,
three crazy twelve year olds,
in the autumn of 1949,
just a wall and a flight of stairs away
from the church sanctuary!

ruthie! she sure could laugh!

ruthie's ma ran a sewing machine
in a clothing factory.
she had a few years to go
before retirement, and talked about
when she'd have more time
to sew anything she wanted,
instead of pants zippers
over and over again.
she'd sit in a big stuffed chair
in her front room on saturday mornings
and crochet doll clothes for ruthie and me;
she'd hold up a little hat or a coat
for us to see, and she'd talk about her job.
she said she didn't mind working
at the factory; she liked the women
she worked with, and sometimes
when the nice foreman was on their shift,
he'd let them talk while they worked.
she kept on crocheting while she talked,
and when she finished a tiny scarf
or a pair of doll mittens
she'd give them to us right away,
and then get up and go in the kitchen to bake.
she smelled of german streusel and hot coffee,
and made apple pancakes for us to eat
while we dressed our dolls.

some saturdays i'd call for ruthie
with my coaster wagon and we'd travel
up her alley to the drinking glass factory
by the railroad tracks.
the people made frosted glasses
with painted flowers on the sides,
and we knew when they threw away the rejects.
so ruthie and i would try to be there
to rescue the best for our mothers.
sometimes we'd find big chunks of cardboard
behind the factory and slide downhill
to the tracks in the gully.
and once we took turns riding down
on an old rocking chair,
'til it broke into pieces.

24

we'd listen for the trains before we slid
and watch and wave at the engineer when
one went by. he'd smile and wave back,
and ruthie would laugh and so would i.

ruthie! she sure could laugh!

on cold days,
ruthie would play the accordion
for her mom and me.
when ruthie played,
her big dark eyes would light up,
her cheeks would get pinker,
and her black hair would curl closer
around her face.
once when she was playing,
her ma told me she looked like her father.
ruthie's dad was killed in a foundry accident
when she was still a baby.
her ma had his picture
on a shelf in the dining room
behind a dried braided palm branch,
and a white candle,
tied with a purple ribbon.
one time i told ruthie she was lucky,
at least there's no yelling and arguing,
if her father was dead.
"ruthie," i said, "you're lucky"
and she answered, "i don't know."

ruthie was a good catholic girl,
said a rosary every day
and got married
at sixteen
birthing five baby girls,
five kids in five years,
one right after the other,
all dark hair, dark eyes
and pink fat cheeks.
she'd wanted to finish high school,
but it didn't work out.

ruthie started with the rest of us
from saint thomas,
at cathedral, downtown on wells street.
it cost money to go to catholic
instead of public high school,
and i remember my father complaining
about the tuition, and my mother arguing
that it was a sin not to send me there.
anyway, we managed because of my father's
welding job at a.o. smith.
but ruthie's ma didn't have enough money
for tuition, from her job,
so she went to see the monsignor
at saint thomas. he told her "never mind,"
he'd "take care of it."
after all, it WAS a sin
not to send your children
to a catholic school.
ruthie's mom didn't want to sin,
so ruthie went to saint john's cathedral,
and when it came time to pay the semester bill,
ruthie's mom went to the church rectory,
but the monsignor just couldn't recall
ever telling her anything like that.
ruthie's ma didn't have the cash.
she couldn't pay the bill.
so sin or no sin,
ruthie was asked to leave saint john's.
her ma enrolled her at washington
on sherman boulevard, but she was lonely.
she didn't know anybody.
she ended up getting pregnant
by the boy across the street
from the drinking glass factory.
had to quit school at sixteen,
and get married,
producing five baby girls,
one right after the other.
five kids in five years,
ruthie was a good catholic girl.

ruthie had to move to the southside
after the wedding.

her husband quit school too,
and the only job he could find
was at a gas station in caledonia.
ruthie missed the old neighborhood
and every chance she could,
she'd make the trip
across the 27th street viaduct
to visit her ma on 32nd street.
she'd always bring the babies along;
her mom said she loved it.
she crocheted baby clothes,
and fed them
homemade applesauce and cookies,
while ruthie played her accordion.

i was a few years behind ruthie
in marriage and babies.
when she was pregnant the fifth time,
it was my third.
my husband was gone a lot.
he said the kids made him nervous.
his job made him tense.
he needed time alone, he said.
anyway ruthie and i
would be on the phone every day,
talking babies and husbands and
never having enough money for anything.
when i was depressed
she could always cheer me up
and have me laughing
with funny things her kids did.
there were times
i'd take care of ruthie's kids,
but i never brought mine
over to her house,
because of her husband.
ruthie said he wasn't a bad man.
he was happy when he fixed cars.
but he'd hit her when he got drunk,
and if the babies got in the way,
they'd get slapped around too.
once, ruthie called the police,
but they told her

there was nothing they could do.
ruthie told me i was lucky
my husband didn't hit me when he got mad,
he'd just stay away from home longer.
"suzie, you're lucky," ruthie said,
and i said, "i don't know."

ruthie jumped off her garage roof
in the eighth month of her last pregnancy.
she phoned to tell me, and when i asked
if she was o.k., she answered,
"yah, nothing happened," and then she laughed.
and one saturday morning, about a year later,
she took the five little pink-cheeked girls
to her mother's house, left them there
eating apple pancakes, and never came back.

i haven't heard from ruthie
in more than 20 years. i hope she's all right.
back then there were no shelters
for battered women, or counseling for spouses.
ruthie survived the only way she could,
and protected her children
by giving them away,
and i can't help thinking of her
whenever i pass through my old neighborhood.
but the ruthie i remember
was my girl friend
when i was growing up;
i think of her face
when she played her accordion.
and sliding downhill
to the railroad tracks.
i think of playing basketball
in the old saint tom's gymnasium,
and i can still see ruthie
sitting on the floor
in a puddle of pee,
laughing and holding the basketball
against her belly.

ruthie!   she sure could laugh!

Boogie Woogie Brother

my big brother
played "boogie woogie"
by ear
on the ancient upright in the parlor

made that piano M O V E
floor dancin' on its wooden caster feet
to "walkin' the dog boogie"

my big brother
took lessons
from the Schaum piano school
'way down on the East Side
just so's he could learn
to read the old songs for our mom

Jimmy rode the North Ave. street car
almost to the lake
on Saturday mornings
when he'd rather be shootin' baskets
at the 31st street school playground

and sometimes
home finally from his lesson
with only half a Saturday left to go
my big brother'd stop
set his basketball 'n peanut butter sandwich
on the red chair in the hall
and peek around the corner
where I'd be cuttin' paper dolls

then he'd grin
and flop down on the old piano bench
to pick a little "boogie woogie"
just
for
me

4

Trying to Turn
a Bad Thing into Good

3:20 p.m.

a worse kind of sad
is the second-shift mom
leaving for work
in the afternoon
through no choice
of her own

just in time
to wave at her kids
getting off the school bus
coming home

   3:25 p.m.

   the man in the life
   of the second-shift woman
   washes cast iron
   from his face and hands
   changes clothes
   and starts on his way
   home from work
   knowing she's already gone

   back and forth they travel
   using every minute
   of the earth's rotation
   her eyes are open
   his are shut
   she's running a machine
   he's figuring out
   another kid emergency
   before he goes to bed
   making decisions
   in his one head
   that could easily use two

they write each other notes
tape record messages
and try not to argue
on the telephone
because it's hell to cry alone

8:00 p.m.

monday through friday
she phones every night
on her 8 o'clock break
from the telephone
in the warehouse
that's the most quiet

then for ten minutes
she listens to her children
grow

says goodbye
hangs up

cries more
'til she cries less
and loves
like a lifetime
full of weekends

3:00 a.m.

second-shift lady
upside-down life
comes home to quiet

let the dog out
let the dog in

eat a little something
take a little bath
climb into a warmed-up bed
to snuggle with
her sleepy first-shift man

A Chant for the Children

let them be
let them become
let them become all
let them become all that
they want to become
a moon a flower a bird a healer
a lover a machinist a farmer a
drummer a sunbeam a carpenter a
rainbow a teacher a rainstorm a
revolutionary becoming a poet
becoming a revolutionary becoming
a child becoming becoming becoming
the children the children the children
let them be like a circle returning
to its center or a picture of a mirror
reflecting a mirror picturing and
mirroring infinitely wanting to learn more
and more never filled never full always
wanting to climb the next hill the next hill
the next hill

Cloud Woman

watching clouds with Linda
  lying on our backs
  on an old green sleeping bag

the clouds are moving fast
  bright, white, gray masses
  changing as we watch

Linda points to one and
  calls it a dolphin
  another is a lamb

we laugh together, daughter and mother
  in love with each other
  and the sky

i feel time moving fast
  like the clouds

i want to grab on to
  this afternoon
  before it slips away

i want to write a poem
  of this, the beginning
  of Linda's sixteenth summer

she's starting her first job
  in less than a week

she's taking a machine shop course
  in her spare time

she talks of jobs and schools
  brothers and tennis shoes

cloud woman Linda
  welcoming change
  like a summer day

cloud woman Linda
  flying into her sixteenth summer
  fly! Linda! fly!

Jim
at twenty

first born.
i grew up with him.
made so many mistakes.
turned around,
tried to fix them.
turned around. started again.
made more mistakes
about mending mistakes;
i get worn out just remembering.

i told him once
that i wanted
the pains of growing up
not just to go away,
but never to start.
i was so wrong.
and sometimes when i look back,
i'm amazed that we ever
made it through.

but we did.
Jim's my son.
but he's a man, grown,
with a factory job,
and an apartment of his own.

i'm still his mother,
but neither of us the same
as we started out.

he was first born
and the first gone
out of the nest.
THE BIG TEST.
and we both passed it
brown hair flying in the wind;

first bird is airborne,
at last.

Tim
at fifteen

a lesson in struggle,
Tim works on Tim,
taking criticism
like Lenin
meant it to be,
with a tear
and a grin.

there is no
stubbornness
in Tim,
except when
he is right,
then watch him
fight to prove it.

understanding
the world
mathematically,
he laughs
at himself,
sometimes trying
to make believe
that 2 plus 2
aren't 4.

laughs
'cause all the while
he know
what
the real answer was,
and
who.

Dan
at thirteen

the youngest in the house,
getting old the fastest.

somehow, Dan's supposed to soak up
all the information
that the other kids
had taught to them.

i'm tired of mothering.

he's tired of being the youngest
in the house
with so much to learn.

he wants to be independent,
but he's lonesome when alone.

he'll fight the notion of being taught,
then turn around and show what he's
just learned.

he's inside outside upside down.

a drummer getting stronger.
a runner slowing down.
he's out of breath,
i'm breathless,
chasing after, up the hill,
and down the other side,

to find we are at least a step beyond
our starting point,

at most, we're better friends.

Tom
July 1960—October 1981

Tom
eighteen
with a slice
sewed up
on your right
index finger
from an accident
on the machine you run
at work

i guarded you
like the rest
of your nestlings
from all the hurts
i could
when you were small

now a machine
took a bite
from your finger
and i couldn't help you
i wasn't even there

i was miles away
just home from working
on a different machine
at a different factory

all i can say
is i'm sorry
it happened

BUT PROUD AS HELL
that you grew up
the way you did

you're the kind
of male worker
i would love
to work beside

helpful
funny
friendly
not racist
or sexist

pro-union
and
"won't take shit"
from the foreman

a bountiful
addition
to the working class!

Stephan
1961—1961

forever a baby
Stephan
your ten-day life
surprised death
and the doctors
you had nine months
to float free
in a mother's ocean
and ten days to live after that
how long is a day
in the life of an infant?
what is the measurement for love?
who asks these questions?
twenty-five years have passed
and I still want the answers

The Man Who Grew
to Be a Father

*For Larry, who helped me learn to
co-parent after years of single parenting*

he's a nice guy
who never intended
to father a child

so he took precautions

still he loved
he lived
and lovers came and left
until a love developed
with five unbiological
contradictions:

he and she and they

quantity became quality

love became loves

and the man who never intended
to father a child

became
the man who grew
to be father

intentionally

Ping Waiting for Pong
or
Everything's Connected

can a mouse f
        a
          l
             l through a crack
in the bathroom ceiling
on the day we had to take
one of our sons to children's court
for attempting to throw an egg at a nazi
in a demonstration
on the day the stereo receiver breaks down
on the day the bathroom shower head
       breaks off
on the day the right headlight goes out
on our car
on the day the rumor starts about a big
       lay-off
coming in november
on the day i have to go to the equal
opportunity people
for more hassle on my two-year-old
sex discrimination suit
on the day after one of our best
unsexist men friends says he's moving
out of town
on the day i get a hurty cold sore
in the corner of my mouth
on the day the upstairs people's mouse
       problem
descended on us downstairs people
through a crack in the bathroom ceiling?

5

Motherdream

i'm flying in a terrible storm
dark clouds on each side
tornado funnels swirl to my left
more purple and gray cyclones
in the distance, directly in my path

a small flock of birds fly around me
five colored ones are being blown in circles
little bird bodies twirling
like circus pinwheels
their blue, green and red feathers
mingle with yellow smoke and gentle down

i begin to feel responsible
i can't help feeling responsible,
not for the storm,
but for the fact that I AM NOT
having difficulty flying
i reach out to one of the birds
it cuddles in my hand
i put it in my brown coat pocket
another flies to me
it too nestles in a coat pocket
another comes to me
and yet another
and i have one pocket left
a tiny green and red bird
brushes my cheek
i take it in my hand
now the last pocket is full of birds
i feel their fast hearts
beating against my body

there's a dirty cold river
rushing below us
now i too am having trouble flying
i'm weighted by some tremendous thing
i cannot understand
i have only five small birds
in my pockets, yet i am heavy
my eyes fill with tears
panic breaks my flight rhythm
i must fly
i must save the birds
i must save myself

we are dangerously close to the water now
one foot touches its wetness
its icy chill shocks me
i use what feels like
the last of my strength
to shoot myself straight upwards
i tangle my coat in a tree branch
hanging over the edge of the river
but at least i'm free of the water

my coat rips

the birds are chirping
i rest in the crook of the tree
gasping for breath
they rest with me

their little eyes
like black seeds
peek out of my pockets
then their heads emerge
then one wing
then the other

like a second hatching

we see leaves through the darkness
this tree is a good tree
the birds wiggle out of my pockets
hopping out to perch on its branches

i'm crying again
and laughing
at the same time
they brush my tears with their wings
it feels good
their feathers are lying flat
calm against their bodies

the wind blows warmer
i hang my coat in the tree
a present for the birds

the sky is pink
the clouds are gone
the wind is dying down

i'm free to fly away

alone

Bird Poem Number One

For my mother Lenares, 1900—1951

My thoughts are like birds
Birds fly in my thoughts
In and out
like the first lines of a poem
but not the rest
They nest in the first lines
and keep me there too long

I am in a nesting time
I wake, I think
I'll write a poem about my mother
I think, I have to get to know her
then I remember that I can't
because she's dead
and bird thoughts flutter
to the ground

But, once I was a baby bird
My mother took me to pretty places
On cold days she would cuddle me
in the folds of her big coat
walking to the streetcar stop
to ride DOWNTOWN!!

Wednesday nights we'd go
to the Rainbow Theater on Lisbon Avenue
and see Betty Grable musicals
and spy shows with Humphrey Bogart
and I would play all the important roles
later on in her bedroom
in front of her big mirror

We'd get free dishes at the Rainbow
Wednesday nights
and when I got to be twelve
the doorman would give me one too
and I would feel proud to be older
and able to give my dish to Momma

I still fly through my old neighborhood
I still live in Milwaukee
My old nests are all over this city
My feathers have fallen in every corner
The old movie show is, of course,
a parking lot

Two of the places I used to live
are barren land with tin cans and broken
     glass
But there are birds flying everywhere
And my mother's wings are still gliding
in and out my mind
all pale purple and dark green embroidery
and every year as I grow older
and learn more about what it means
to be a mother bird, with baby birds
pulling at my feathers
I know my mother better all the time

Menopause Poem

getting older
smiling through 47 years
i cook eggs for breakfast this morning
taking a necessary day off from the factory
i bite into my toast while thumbing through
OUR BODIES OURSELVES
chapter 17
Menopause
then i have to go to the bathroom
and get my partial plate
that i left in its little blue plastic box
soaking overnight
in baking soda
in the cabinet under the sink
because without all my teeth
the toast in my mouth
is too difficult to chew
and i laugh with myself
seeing myself holding a piece of bitten toast
reading about menopause
and hunting for false teeth
because what i'm looking for
in chapter 17
is how to best keep on making love at 47
with a vagina that tends to dry a bit
and good old OUR BODIES book
answers with
saliva
KY jelly
and a loving partner
so as soon as i finish my eggs
i'm on the way to the drugstore
to get the one i don't have

Doris's Poem
Allis Chalmers Tractor Shop

the machine she runs
is a washer as big as a semi-trailer
no clothes go in it
hot chemical water
fumes from its dark openings
at both ends

a conveyor belt travels through it
on first shift it takes two workers
to tend the washer

on second for the last 20 years
there's Doris

she loads one end
with 15 or 20
tractor engine parts
each steel piece
weighing an average
of 25 pounds

she walks around to the other side
waiting for them to emerge
hot and steamy
like boiled steel cabbages

she sprays the remaining dirt and chips
blowing in their bolt holes
with a high pressure air hose

the hose tries to pull from her
    gloved hand
like an electric eel

she won't let it
she has control

she's Doris on the washer

Doris could retire in 2 years
but she doesn't plan to

she thinks she'll work
as long as they let her

she has 2 kids at home
teenagers... you know how they eat

she just saved enough for a down payment
on a house
she's always wanted to go to California
to visit her oldest daughter

she won't retire yet

Doris lights a cigarette
it's 8 p.m.
second shift lunchtime
sweat shines on her forehead
her gray hair is wet with it

she wipes her face
with a clean shop rag
she puffs her cigarette
sitting at the lunch table
in the women's locker room
an empty tuna can
is her ash tray

she comments on the heat
of the summer night
the stupid foreman
and the amount of work
she's NOT going to do

it's her strength
it's her strength
that I need to learn

it's her strength

Womyn's Reading Night

for the Feminist Writers Guild,
Milwaukee Chapter

brown gold
sun orange
sucking sounds
in a circle
of womb strength
in a circular room
strength
breathing
in and out
giving
in and out
candle light
apple poems
womyn
and a baby
singing
and cooing
to each other
sucking each
into each
other
renewing
womyn's sounds
sensual
precious
sympathetic
and
strong as
mothers' milk

And Part of Me Is Momma

I can hear the scratching
of her pen
writing in my school notebook
on the dining room table

I can hear her coming
when I called
from my bed
late at night

Momma come
tell me a story
come rub my back
come to me and

she would come

telling me stories
of her childhood
on the farm
stories of her young girl days
and her best friend
Rosie Dupkie
and her high button shoes
that she took off to run
in the warm wet country mud

I could feel her toes
squiggle in its thickness

I could see the farm house
through her eyes
through her words

easing this city child
to sleep

and Momma
did you go back to write?

and part of me is Momma

Sleep of the Moth

wings fold
ears plug
antennas retract
little preparations done
she clings
to a dark
corner
of her world
slightly
vibrating
to the drone
of day
she fades away
third shift sleeper
in the center
of the sun
the sleep
of the moth
has come

Poem for the Nicaraguan Mothers

the color of
poems
the color of
green vines growing
in a land
the color of truth
in the night
the color of dark
they come to you
calling out words
the color of truth
in a time when truth
is too terrible to be heard
too terrible to be told
in a time when truth
is the color of
green vines growing
in the night
to be told
to be told
naked in the middle of the night
to be told
your son is dead
your daughter is dead
children soldiers
in a war for freedom
to be told
the children
the children
dead dead
Miguel
Rosa
Carlos
Tomás
presente

they come to us
the mothers
the mothers
gathering poems
in the middle of the night
gathering words
the color of truth
in the midday sun
they come to us
shouting REVOLUTION
for the dead children
their lives the color
of green vines growing
the color of truth
the color of worth
the color of revolution
the color of life
turning death around
in a time when truth must be told
in a time when
truth and poems
and a country's future
are the color of
green vines growing

Eden's Motel

for Rose and Tom

1

i am a survivor i
sleep with
clenched fists jaws
tightened against
themselves
guarding dreams and
memories

one son is dead two
mothers are dead
as i awake in eden
to sit
on a gray toilet
and write
crazy words

2

while in the other
room through the dim of a
Chicago morning
my loving comrade sleeps
the sleep
of an injured gentle dragon a
motherless child a
father whose son is
lost in the quiet screaming of
dreams inside his gut

3

still i write to
keep alive to
survive
with teeth
clenching and
unclenching
fingernails raw from
picking at each
other waiting to see people
who ask how
i am and
hope my answer is all
right so
that they can
know how soon their
answer would be the same to
the same
question

but these days my
answer is
not yet all
right

my answer is
a dream less feared
than reality
for my dream holds
five babies
reality
four

my womb is gone
reality lives

i am a survivor i
sleep with
clenched fists
guarding

6

First Poem from
My New Job on the Railroad

is Sylvester
not yet ready
for retirement
walking up to me
third week on the job

Sylvester
smiling and nodding
watching me
nervously operate
the wheel bore machine

Sylvester
waiting for me
to finish the wheel

then taking his huge hand
from its hiding place
behind his back

opening his fist
to show
a railroad spike
brand new
shiny
with "Sue machinist
wheel bore...1978"
hand painted
in yellow railroad
marker

thank you Sylvester
for this
first
poem

Artichoke Poem

take a hungry person
who forgot to bring her lunch
to work today

and then take an artichoke
last night
in the hands of Augie
from Sicily

who cut it
soaked it
in lemon juice
boiled it
spiced it
onioned and egged it
crumbed it
mixed and fried it

then created a sandwich
that he offers
to share with me
this morning

put them all together
and give thanks
to artichokes
and Augie
the machinist helper
who keeps the train wheels
rolling down the tracks

Veteran

1

Eddie on the mounter
Vietnam tattooed on his heart
thanks to Agent Orange and Uncle Sam
glides sure and easy
as his stride in the wheel shop
what's the hurry!
work is an 8 hour battle
of wheels to be mounted
on shiny axles
watch the tonnage on the chart
light or heavy
depending on machinist skill
diameters of wheel centers and axle fits
the amount of white lead paint applied
and Eddie on the press pedal
rolling sure and easy on the surface
two wars simmering inside

2

Eddie on the mounter
keeps the foreman dog at bay
like his crew-cut counterpart in Vietnam
displays his Attitude
like a steely mask of strength
to the leery sergeant of a foreman
white as lead paint
dripping on the wheelshop floor
racist as a klanner
but afraid of Eddie's calm
scans machine gun fire in Eddie's eyes
declines to comment on production
or the length of Eddie's breaks
feels the fire stab
the nape of his red neck
as he tries not to tear-ass by

3

Eddie off the mounter
veteran of at least two wars
changes like Wisconsin weather
from calm to gusts at 60 miles per hour
peeling rubber in a Friday parking lot
bound for forgetting
with friends and a beer or two
those Vietnam and railroad time bomb
blues

You Can't Go Back to Work
in the Middle of a Card Game

playing poker
for dimes
at lunchtime
in the wheel shop

we are low-key
competition players
coins changing hands
as quick as a clock's tick

no cut-throat here
we laugh
yell
swear
slap cards on the table

and finish one last fast game
right into the blast
of the noon whistle

Sisters
Milwaukee Road

now don't get me wrong!
the guys i work with
are a good old bunch

it's just that sometimes
when i look around
and see no one like me
i think of two
who used to be here
in this factory full of men

two other women
one two three we were
sisters in hard hats
with bobbie pins and wrenches
in our pockets
sharing those working women's
special blues

like sisters we were
trading stories of different jobs
laughing crying together
in the foreman's tiny bathroom
where our lockers stood

like sisters we were
and there was nothing like it!

now one's gone
one's laid off
and there's only me again

but don't get me wrong!
the guys i work with
are a good old bunch

it's just that sometimes
when i look around...

With Love
from the Wheel Shop

for Larry

we are a poem being created
we are writing ourselves
on a clean piece of paper
with love
as the first word
and honesty
the second
with the rest
changing
like a new sound
from your banjo

we are more than two
we are sudden leaps
and slow dances
and a saturday night
scary movie
wanted or not
thrown in for excitement

we know the lull is over
the storm subsiding
fear being conquered
by rainbows

what was isn't
what is
is becoming

we are new
we are not wanting
we are not waiting
we are moving

the poem will be a good one

i can feel it

Poem for Jenny

I never worked with you
but your husband
runs a machine next door to me

I never spent time alone with you
tho we all went out for fish fries
on two different Friday nights

I never worked with you
but I feel as if I know you
through the eyes of a husband
who speaks of you with pride and love
and years of sharing

I never worked with you
but I know how it is to go to work
and stand on feet all day
that scream for you to sit down

know how it is to wonder
if the kids will be all right
when they get home from school
and you're not there

how to birth five babies
in this crazy world
and give them all of yourself
wishing it could be more

wishing you were more
wishing you could be
in at least two places
at the same time

I never worked with you
but I know the sister worker feelings
we both share

know we're strong and proud
and have a right to be

and, Jenny, I know you

Vacation

back from vacation
trickling streams
cool rushing waterfalls
Canadian sunsets
only a dream
now that reality
is spinning
in front of me
in this damn machine
two tons of train axle
with wheels attached
making the only breeze
to be felt on my face
in this 95 degree fahrenheit
August MONDAY

please... pa-leeezz
don't anybody mention
proletarian discipline to me
today

Verona

worked the same shift
for one beautiful week
shared days as close
as two working women can get
changed clothes and peed together
in the tiny foreman's bathroom
tried to pack one week
as full of sisterhood as possible
gulped each other down
in huge bites
and hugged the first time we met
right there in the wheel shop
in other words
we got to know each other
real fast
we had to

now she comes in
a half hour early
for second shift
so we can at least touch thoughts
tells me she doesn't know
how she'd get along without me
sixty now and seeing the light
at the end of the retirement tunnel
but the night and the tunnel are long for her
only woman on second shift
getting tired of it all
I tell her the same
that these half hours
are what keep me going
we are two canaries
in a mine shaft
huddling for safety
sniffing for smoke
waiting to see the light of day

Earl's Poems

1

on a good day
Earl runs the lathe next to me

spins those train axles in ol' number seven
    with ease

cuts coils of shiny blue metal chips
like little fat slinky spring toys

makes number seven hummmmmmmmmm with
    delight
when he's on a roll

then in late afternoon
he'll slow down the day

put another axle in the machine
turn it on
and "cut air"
while he reads the sports page

'cause Earl--he'll NEVER NEVER bust
    the rate

2

a bad day's when Earl's put workin'
    somewhere else
and the guy that NOBODY likes runs
    number seven!

3

Earl broke me in on number eight
        journal lathe
a fifteen foot long sucker of a machine
that cuts the parts of train axles
that stick out from the wheels

one and a half tons of trouble
spinning around in a blur
looks like a giant's weightlifting dumbbells
I mean
the whole damn thing gets put into the lathe

and Earl, he shows me what to do
he says: "no woman ever ran this job before
don't worry you'll do just fine"
says to take my time...be safe
don't worry 'bout production
then Earl...he be so calm...so calm
he make even MY nerves relax
and he was right
in time...I did just fine

4

Earl and I talk of old times
growin' up in the '40s
him in Shreveport
walkin' barefoot on hot Louisiana road dust

me in Milwaukee barefoot on the summer
        sidewalks

both of us hatin' shoes
both of us likin' to walk barefoot in the
        summer
'cause shoes hurt our feet

but at least I could go try shoes on with
        my momma
at Branovan's or Sears on Fondulac

Earl, his momma had to draw feet pictures

outline Earl's and his brother's and sister's
        feet on paper
and take it to town to the shoe store
'cause back then Black people weren't
        allowed
to try stuff on 'fore they bought it from
        the white stores

Earl's momma took string and measured
        waists, arms and legs
of all her kids with loving care
brought the string lengths shopping
        with her

Earl says he saw little Black kids get beat
just for holdin' up a pair of pants to
        themselves

Earl and I talk of old times

but not all of them
good

Family Man

1

farmer of fields
and diesel wheels
Big John
runs a machine
that's been here
longer than the oldest guy
remembers

he drives 45 miles
sunrise and sunset
from sweet smelling
country breezes
to Milwaukee Road smoke

back and forth
dropping off his partner
of 27 years
at HER factory job
and picking her up
for the tired happy ride home
to their five grown kids
and now two grandchildren

27 years of family
farm and factory
for Big John
a tough and gentle man
who's not afraid to say
he loves his wife

2

when John and Jenny's
oldest was born
he was laid off

Jenny had a one week rest
then she was at a punch press
in Milwaukee
with John at home
caring for the baby
and a farm
not to mention
having supper ready
when she got home

John tells of taking
his little bundled daughter
along on the tractor seat
with a baby bottle
packed in his lunch box
and diapers on the dashboard

when he got called back
to the railroad second shift
they managed
a whirl of two worlds
first and second shifters
traveling to town
passing their days and nights
until the weekends

and John says
Jenny waited up for him

John's not afraid to say
he loves his wife

3

like the wizard
in Oz land

John makes that
old wheel-bore machine
roar with creation

using both hands
at the same time
for the dials and levers

standing leg-spread for balance

hard hat screwed on tight

chips flying like popcorn
exploding from
a hot pan

like the wizard
in Oz land

John's in command
of the situation

4

John's potatoes
are grown
with sun and love
and rain
and good Wisconsin soil

no bug spray
touches their
beautiful brown skin

when you boil up
some of John's potatoes
and butter 'em on your plate

you bite into
a memory
of how potatoes
used to taste

Union Man

the day
the letter came
from management
beginning with
an affirmative answer
to a union grievance
and ending with
a stern command
that workers
be on time
and never never
leave early

Don the machinist
president of his union
a 30-year man
too young to retire
left work early
for the second time
in his career

the first being
two years ago
the day he went
to the doctor
who put him in
the hospital
for by-pass surgery

on the day
the letter came
from management
Don told the foreman
he was leaving
and grinned
as he walked out
the factory door
at 1:30 in the afternoon
of the birth
of his first grandchild

7

1980

we come
to work
every day
every day
like the other
feeling
robbed
and cheated
and ready
to burst
like a
train wheel
mounted
on the wrong
axle
a quarter ton
of steel
stretched
too tight
a wheel
waiting
to explode
at a temperature
change
or a bump
in the track
we are people
ready to
burst

Bacon Lettuce Bankruptcy

the time we have left together
this bunch of men and I
these brawly burly hearts
beating irregularly
worry tense with job insecurity
plus or minus by-pass surgery
and high blood pressure
these railroad men
with no experience at new job searches
having never even made out an application
when they started here as kids 30 years ago
these working class giants
watching retirement dreams dissolve
like solvent eating into grease
the time we have left together is spent
tasting the sale of this hundred year old
      railroad
talking about it at every coffee lunch or
      toilet break
work/layoff/bankruptcy
work/layoff/bankruptcy
like a stale sandwich from the vendor truck
we're sick to death of it

Fever

only woman
working these last days
my stomach is burning
my nerve ends electric   raw
men come to me
crying tears never used before
the machines we run
are being dug up and dragged
out the doors
like giant trees
roots clinging to our legs
we watch them leave
tied to flat-bed trucks
bound for shops
with newer roofs
walls without holes
and the men come
pouring out their nightmares
telling me things they were taught
they cannot tell each other
a woman machinist
is a woman first
to these traditional men
so when I speak of Capitalist greed and
        insanity
my words simply fall to the factory floor
with the shiny steel chips
the men want my female car
not my ideology
but for every man
every story of family arguments
suicidal thoughts
nervous conditions
divorce
children not going to school
for every job lost forever
in company computers
for every terrible tear
every drunken drugged Sunday night
and industrial accident

caused by fear of tomorrow
for every worker here
my anger rises
like mercury in a thermometer
I am trying to register
as accurately as possible
trying to record this communal fever
we are burning
burning
burning
Capitalists
beware!

Denial

and some deny it all
men who can measure
the thickness of metal
by thousandths of an inch
refuse to believe
the railroad will ever close
refuse to admit their futures
will ever change
come to work in creaking buildings
every day
change to their workclothes
start the machines
and stare into space
surrounded by
sparking blue hot metal chips

Notes from the Electric Shop

old John
blind in one eye
wears sunglasses
in the dark shop
packs his memories
in boxes labeled
Shorham Yards
crates up diesel engine parts
like he's saying good-bye
to old friends
turns from his tool bench
caressing a small steel coupling
hesitates a moment
flings it in the trash bin
with a vengeance

for 20 years these parts
were molded to his hands
as he assembled diesels
engines that pulled freight trains
through snow and sunshine
now he packs them
for other workers
in another factory
to open like christmas presents

they're closing the Milwaukee shops
it's on to Minnesota
John tapes shut the last box
looks out what has been
his window all these years
watches the wrecking ball
bang down the building next door
"piss on it" he mumbles
as he slams the window
and pours himself a cup of coffee
from his dented thermos
"piss on it!"

The Means of Production

they're taking John's machine away

for 25 years he's run it
for 25 years he's been part of it
his arms and hands connected to the levers
extensions of a powerful machine
a powerful man
creating diesel train wheels
his sweat mingling with its oil
every workday for 25 years
he's spent more time with it
than he has with his wife
he says
got a doctor appointment for Saturday
doesn't feel right
he says
a man who's never been sick a day in his life

they're taking John's machine away

they own it
he knows

Puppies

Big Wheels
says Don the machinist
are what little puppies
piss on
and a puppy at the railroad
these days
would have no trouble
finding spots to piss

SUE DORO, daughter of a homemaker mother and welder father, was born April 17, 1937 in Berlin, Wisconsin and spent her first 48 years in Milwaukee. She bore six children; one died ten days after birth, one at age 21.

Silenced by years of housewifing, Sue was opened up again by divorce (1969-74), the women's movement, left politics and jobs in nontraditional fields. She was a machinist at Hellwig (1974-75), at Allis Chalmers (1975-78), and at the Milwaukee Road Railroad (1978-85). She was also a union steward and strike counselor in Local 248 United Auto Workers and the Safety Committee captain in the wheel shop of the Milwaukee Road; especially important among these years is 1985 when the bankrupt Milwaukee Road was sold without regard for the workers and their lives. After early retirement, Sue moved to California and found work as Executive Director of Tradeswomen, Inc., a grass roots, nonprofit organization of women working in blue collar jobs, which puts out a magazine by the same name.

Her poems have found a wide audience, from mainstream to worker to unemployed; in 1977 she received first prize in the national UAW writers contest for an article on International Women's Day. She met Meridel Le Sueur in Chicago in 1978 and has "corresponded shared connected and loved ever since."

AMMO, United Auto Workers International Union,
2457 East Washington Street, Indianapolis, IN
56201
BROOMSTICK (magazine by and for women over 40),
3543 18th Street, #3, San Francisco, CA 94110
THE FIVE PETALED BLOSSOM, c/o P.O. Box 92606,
Milwaukee, WI 53202
FORWARD MOTION, P.O. Box 1884, Jamaica Plain,
MA 02130
M. MAGAZINE FOR GENTLE MEN, Box 313, 306 North
Brooks Street, Madison, WI 53715
MILL HUNK HERALD, 916 Middle Street, Pittsburgh,
PA 15212
THE MACHINIST, International Association of
Machinists and Aerospace Workers,
1300 Connecticut Avenue, Washington, DC 20036
PRIMIPARA, Box 371, Oconto, WI 54143
TALKIN' UNION, Box 5349, Takoma Park, MD 20912
TRADESWOMAN MAGAZINE, P.O. Box 40664, San
Francisco, CA 94190
WOMEN: A JOURNAL OF LIBERATION, 3028
Greenmount Avenue, Baltimore, MD 21218

For information about other books available
through Midwest Villages & Voices, please write
to us at 3220 10th Avenue South, Minneapolis, MN
55407.